GERMAN
à la Cartoon

Edited by
Albert H. Small, Ph.D.

with the assistance of
Nan Ronsheim

PASSPORT BOOKS
a division of *NTC Publishing Group*
Lincolnwood, Illinois USA

Dedicated to
Barbara
Our Resident Linguist

1993 Printing

Published by Passport Books, a division of NTC Publishing Group.
©1991 by NTC Publishing Group, 4255 West Touhy Avenue,
Lincolnwood (Chicago), Illinois 60646-1975 U.S.A.
Manufactured in the United States of America.

2 3 4 5 6 7 8 9 VP 9 8 7 6 5 4

Contents

A—Careful!—Word in Advance

When you start to study German you may be impressed with some of the similarities you see between German and English. We might consider them family resemblances. German could be called a cousin of English, because they have a largely common origin.

In the tides of migration, conquest and settlement that swept across Europe in the centuries after the fall of the Roman empire, people from areas where German is spoken today made their way to England. Their language—Anglo-Saxon—may be considered a parent of the language we speak today.

But the differences between modern German and modern English are marked. This is not only because of the years that geography has separated the two areas, but because English today contains many words that the church and scholars brought from Latin and the Normans brought from France.

Yet if you look at many of the basic one- and two-syllable words in English you will see how similar their German counterparts are:

ENGLISH	GERMAN
and	und
can	kann
father	Vater
field	Feld
friend	Freund
have	haben
here	hier
home	Heim
house	Haus
man	Mann
market	Markt
mother	Mutter

German is the language of middle Europe, spoken not only in Germany, Austria and Switzerland (the most widely spoken of Switzerland's four languages), but also by substantial populations in western Poland, Czechoslovakia, Hungary, Yugoslavia, and northern Italy.

As a matter of fact, German languages include Dutch and Flemish, descended from common roots with standard German, but much changed in spoken form from the German that has become standard farther east.

German-speaking people have played a major role in the development of the United States. In 1683 thirteen Mennonite families came to America in search of religious freedom and founded—appropriately—Germantown, Pennsylvania.

German-speaking populations had grown to such an extent by the mid-1700s that even Benjamin Franklin was alarmed: "Why should Pennsylvania, founded by the English, become a colony of ALIENS, who will shortly be so numerous as to Germanize us instead of our Anglifying them."

Franklin need not have worried. German influences helped build the country, but what they produced became part of the country. German immigrants originated the Conestoga wagon, invented the Kentucky rifle, built the Brooklyn Bridge and introduced those ever-popular blue jeans.

Signs of our German heritage still remain. Today it is estimated that three million Americans have German as their first language, and 50 million Americans have at least partial German ancestry. Our favorite fast food is called the hamburger after Hamburg, Germany. St. Louis and Milwaukee, the country's beer capitals, still celebrate German seasonal festivals. Bismarck, North Dakota, retains the name of the nineteenth-century German chancellor, selected in a bid to lure German investment for the transcontinental railroad. The Amish, or "Pennsylvania Dutch" (German), retain many traditional customs even to the extent of plowing their fields and driving to town only in horse-drawn vehicles.

Beginners studying German may think of it as a rather formal language. There are several reasons.

First of all, Every Noun is CAPITALIZED. Even the kitchen sink (Ausguss). And the wastebasket (Papierkorb). And the doorknob (Türgriff). Even the paper clip (Büroklammer).

Secondly, the verbs: typically they are at the end of the sentence, and sometimes the sentence is long. An American has claimed that he labored through nine volumes of the writings of Immanuel Kant (the famous German philosopher) only to find the verb in the tenth! And verbs can "come apart." A boy asking a girl for a date may say (literally) "Go you with me out" ("Gehen Sie mit mir aus"), the verb "ausgehen" meaning to go out.

And finally the L—O—N—G words. German spelling loves to crowd as many as three consonants in front of one vowel. And to string ideas together to make one word. For example, "zusammenbringen" means "to bring together"—in this example, English and German use the same number of letters, but German lumps them together in one word. "Spring fever" becomes "Frühjahrsmüdigkeit" in German. "Army drill ground" combines "Truppen" (army), "Übungs" (drill) and "Platz" (place) into one word: "Truppenübungsplatz."

Words also come in families. A patient is a "Kranke" in German (no wisecracks please!). A hospital is a "Krankenhaus." A "Krankenschein" is a medical certificate, and a "Krankenschwester" is a nurse.

Sometimes the words sound almost poetic to us: "Klingelknopf" is a doorbell. "Baumschützer" are tree protectors—that is, environmentalists. A "Schalldämpfer" (literally "sound damper") is a silencer, and the Lord's Prayer becomes "Vaterunser" (literally "our father") in German.

The cartoons in this book were chosen because the humor can be translated into English from German. For example, in German, as in English, the cartoonist can ridicule the boyfriend who calls on his girl with "serious intentions" on April Fool's Day!

But note well: the literal translation into English and the "Everyday English" caption at the bottom of the page can be quite different. In effect, what we have sometimes done is to recaption the cartoon the way an American editor might in adapting a German cartoon for an American newspaper or magazine. This not only improves the joke, but often sharply illustrates the difference between German and English conversational idioms. And that's the purpose of this book. To help take you away from the routine rules of syntax and vocabulary, and bring you out to the world of people speaking German in ordinary circumstances.

Why choose humor as a learning aid? Obviously because humor is an enjoyable way of getting anything done. But more than that, the key to learning is memory—and for almost everybody there is nothing more memorable than a really good joke.

So please don't blame us if you remember the German word for "to fly" by identifying it with a jet passenger who has his own wings. Or if you associate the word for "watchdog" with the sign on a kennel: "On vacation—do your own barking." Or if the German phrase for "eat more beef" suggests a pig with a picket sign. Not to mention the German word for "gasoline" and the aggrieved motorist who wants to know why the price is up when the oil companies dump it in the sea for free.

A Technical Comment—or Two

Learning a language can be fun—especially when it helps you understand the punch line of a joke or the conversation at a get-together. But let's face it, learning a language can also get complicated. In this book we're going to try to keep in as much of the fun as we can, and burden you with a minimum of the complications.

Basically, the vocabulary provided in this book is an aid to understanding the cartoons. So you will excuse us if we don't give you all the *possible* translations of a German word— just the ones that relate to the material at hand. For example, the German word "Holz" might refer to a "mast," but we translate it as "flag" because that's the term we use in English for the markers on the ski run shown in the cartoon.

And we won't bother translating the words you can figure out for yourself, even in cases where the spelling differs somewhat from the spelling in English. But please be alert for the differing ways in which similar words can be used in German. For example, the German word "Mann" can refer to a man or a husband. But "Mensch" also means man, or person, or a human being, or, in the plural, mankind.

Incidentally, we've used some fairly obvious abbreviations: *n.* for noun, *adj.* for adjective, *adv.* for adverb, *v.* for verb, *inf.* for infinitive. Gender is indicated by *m.* for masculine, *f.* for feminine, and *n.* for neuter. To help you recognize a verb in other usages, we add the infinitive form (when the infinitive isn't used in the cartoon caption) along with the verb form that appears.

To avoid cluttering up the vocabulary list under each cartoon, we've given you three sections that handle the most common words. **Pronouns** are an especially important part of everyday speech, so you will want to be familiar with all the common ones. Then, the **Three Important Verbs**—German for "to be," "to have" and "to become"—are important for themselves and as helper verbs, just as in English. You will want to recognize their various forms on sight. Finally, **The Little**

Words are the ones that link together ordinary speech—words like *the, but, now,* and so forth. Rather than repeatedly listing them every time a cartoon caption uses them, we've brought them together in this list to encourage you to make sure they are a basic part of your German vocabulary.

Pronouns*

I. PERSONAL PRONOUNS

Singular

HE:	der Mann	(the man)	er
	den Mann	(*Acc.*)	ihn
	dem Mann	(*Dat.*)	ihm
SHE:	die Frau	(the woman)	sie
	die Frau	(*Acc.*)	sie
	der Frau	(*Dat.*)	ihr
IT:	das Kind	(the child)	es
	das Kind	(*Acc.*)	es
	dem Kind	(*Dat.*)	ihm

Plural

THEY:	die Männer, die Frauen, die Kinder	(*Nom.*)	sie
	die Männer (etc.)	(*Acc.*)	sie
	den Männern (etc.)	(*Dat.*)	ihnen

First and Second Pronouns

	I	**You**	**We**	**You (*pl.*)**
Nom.:	ich	du	wir	ihr, Sie
Acc.:	mich	dich	uns	euch, Sie
Dat.:	mir	dir	uns	euch, Ihnen

II. INDEFINITE PRONOUNS

nichts = nothing, alles = everything, etwas = something

---

*Abbreviations used in this section:

Nom.	Nominative case (subject of the sentence)
Acc.	Accusative case (object of the sentence)
Dat.	Dative case (indirect object)
Gen.	Possessive case

III. RELATIVE PRONOUNS (also the definite article)

German has masculine, feminine and neuter as well as plural
relative pronouns in all four cases. These are very similar to
the forms of the definite article:

	Masc.	**Fem.**	**Neut.**	**Plur.**	
Nom.:	der	die	das	die	(who, which)
Acc.:	den	die	das	die	(whom, which)
Dat.:	dem	der	dem	*denen*	(to whom, to which)
Gen.:	*dessen*	*deren*	*dessen*	*deren*	(whose, of which)

The five forms in italics are UNLIKE the definite article.

The Relative Pronoun WER (who)

Wissen Sie, *wer* das ist?   Do you know who that is?

Acc.:	wen	(whom)
Dat.:	wem	(whom)
Gen.:	wessen	(whose)

The Relative Pronoun WAS (what)

Wissen Sie, *was* das ist?   Do you know what that is?

Acc.:   was   (what)   also: an was = *woran*
Dat.:   nach was = *wonach*

IV. REFLEXIVE PRONOUNS

English uses the suffixes -self or -selves in forming reflexive
pronouns (myself, himself, themselves, etc.). German has
reflexive pronouns that are identical with the personal
pronouns in all but the third person singular and plural:

ihn, sie, es = personal pronoun
sich   reflexive pronoun
sie, Sie   = personal pronoun
sich   reflexive pronoun

Examples: Er erschoss *sich* (Acc.) (He shot himself.)

Er kaufte *sich* etwas (Dat.) (He bought himself
    something.)

Sie erinnerten *sich* (Pl.) (They reminded
    themselves.)

Three Important Verbs

These verbs are important not only by themselves but also as auxiliary verbs (Hilfsverben) used with other verbs to form certain tenses, as we do in English when, for example, we say "I *have* seen him."

HABEN (to have)	**SEIN (to be)**	**WERDEN (to become)**
Present	**Present**	**Present**
ich habe	ich bin	ich werde
du hast	du bist	du wirst
er, sie, es hat	er, sie, es ist	er, sie, es wird
wir haben	wir sind	wir werden
ihr habt, Sie haben	ihr seid, Sie sind	ihr werdet, Sie werden
sie haben	sie sind	sie werden
Past	**Past**	**Past**
ich hatte	ich war	ich wurde
du hattest	du warst	du wurdest
er, sie, es hatte	er, sie, es war	er, sie, es wurde
wir hatten	wir waren	wir wurden
ihr hattet, Sie hatten	ihr wart, Sie waren	ihr wurdet, Sie wurden
sie hatten	sie waren	sie wurden
Perfect	**Perfect**	**Perfect**
gehabt:	gewesen:	geworden:
ich habe gehabt	ich bin gewesen	ich *bin* geworden

Most German verbs take *haben* as their auxiliary in forming the *present perfect* tense. However, intransitive verbs expressing a motion or change of condition require *sein*. The *future tense* is made up of the present tense of the auxiliary verb *werden* plus an infinitive. For example, "Ich werde morgen fahren" (I will go out tomorrow).

The Little Words

aber	but
ach	also
am (an dem)	at (preposition)
au	Oh! ouch!
auch	also
auf	on
aus	from, out of
bei	at
bitte	please
da	there
denn	then
der, die, das	the
doch	yet, indeed
ein, einen	a, an, one
für	for
Herr	Mr.
im	in
ja	yes
kein	no
mal	for once (adverb), one day
mit	with
na?	well?
nach	after, to
nein	no
nicht	not

noch	yet, still
nun	now
nur	only
oder	or
schon	already
so	thus, as
um	around, about, for, in order to
und	and
von	of, from
was	what
wann	when
wenn	if
wer	who
wie	how
zu	to

Introducing . . . the Artists!

Dietmar Grosse was born in Leipzig (East Germany) just over 40 years ago, but grew up in West Germany. He served briefly in the merchant marine.

He studied graphic design in Munich and became art director for various German advertising agencies. But advertising was not to be his chosen career. Instead, in 1979 he earned his license as a private pilot and began publishing aviation cartoons. His work attracted attention in the form of one-man exhibitions and a number of books published by major German publishing houses.

In 1984 he obtained qualification as a stunt flier, and became a regular contributor to *Pilot und Flugzeug* (*Pilot and Plane*).

His cartoons are regularly exhibited in Germany and abroad, and appear frequently in technical journals. He is currently at work on additional books.

Heinz Langer was born in 1937 in Heidenheim (West Germany) and moved to Munich in 1972, where he still resides.

In *Cartoon and Satire,* one of a series of books honoring German and foreign cartoonists, Langer is described as somewhat of a hermit, not interested in worldly goods or money, who ambled through a variety of unimportant jobs before taking up cartooning. He even published one of his books himself, it is said, so as not to be bothered by his editors' comments.

After he arrived in Munich, Langer's work began to appear regularly in a great number of newspapers and magazines, French as well as German. In addition to general-interest publications, his cartoons regularly appear in the *Medical Tribune,* and the examples in this book show how sharp his pen can be when depicting what goes on in the doctor's office!

In addition to two children's books, Langer has published *Langer's Landleben* (*Langer's Life in the Country*), *Langer Samstag* (*A Long Saturday*) and *Friday, February 13, 1982.*

One indication of the international reach of cartoon humor: Langer received an award from the Japanese newspaper *Yomiuri Shimbun.*

Horst von Möllendorff was born in 1906 in Frankfurt/Oder (East Germany), but his parents moved to Berlin in 1914. Descendent of a family of Prussian nobility, Möllendorff received a military education. He discovered his ability to draw during an extended period of recovery in a military hospital during the First World War.

His specialty as a cartoonist developed over the next ten years. His first cartoon appeared in *Brummbär* (*Growler*), a supplement to the *Berliner Morgenpost* (*Berlin Morning Post*) and his cartoons appeared regularly in the *Berliner Illustrierte Nachtausgabe* (*Illustrated Berlin Night Edition*). His regular feature in the latter paper was captioned "My Sunday Experience."

Möllendorff created a cartoon character known as "Smily"— a laughing face without a nose—which he considers his inner portrait. His book of drawings entitled *Berlin Without Words* illustrating Berlin after World War II went through several editions; the Berlin Wall, which didn't exist at the time of original publication, was added to a later edition. The famous West German magazine *Der Stern* featured his weekly cartoon of "Kessi," a smart German girl, for 15 years.

Möllendorff also produced three cartoon films, one of which, *Weather-worn Melody,* was a prize-winning cultural film. More recently (in 1987) he was honored with the Order of Merit of the Federal German Republic.

One of his hobbies is the creation of original costumes for carnival time.

Although born in Lithuania, **Aribert Nesslinger (Ane)** has lived in Berlin for the last 50 years. From his Russian mother and East Prussian father he says he has inherited a "vodka-tolerant liver."

What makes a humor cartoonist? Nesslinger says three
years on the Russian front during World War II, four
war wounds and five years in Russian prisons were his
preparations.

Bureaucrats are favorite targets for Nesslinger's cartoons.
He blames this on his "faulty relationship with German
officials." Yet Americans will see this as a mark of true
internationalism.

Nesslinger's work has appeared in just about every German
newspaper and feature publication. For the past 30 years
most of his cartoons have appeared in Berlin daily papers, and
his contract with the evening *Der Abend* goes back 22 years.

But the Nesslinger touch goes beyond cartoons. He has
written humorous travel reports (including one on New York)
and scripts for films and television. He has also directed
short film comedies and appeared in four of them as the main
actor.

A confirmed "Berliner," Nesslinger received the "Goldenen
Malstift" (Golden Pencil) award in that city, and came in first
in a cartoonists' competition sponsored by the Federal
Statistics Office.

Nesslinger has been married but is separated from his wife
("I prefer a glass in my hand to a wife in my arms") and
has a grown daughter.

Karl-Heinz Schoenfeld was born in Oranienburg, Germany
just over 60 years ago. Art was his heritage: both parents were
painters. Karl-Heinz studied engineering, and served an
apprenticeship as a precision mechanic at Zeiss-Ikon, the
camera and lens-making company.

After World War II he was able to turn to art. He studied
at the "Hochschule für Bildende Künste" and also under the
famous painter Pechstein. While there, one of his teachers
noticed his aptitude for cartooning, and advised him to exploit
this talent.

Although Schoenfeld's cartoons in this volume are humorous, he is primarily a political cartoonist. His cartoons have crossed the Atlantic Ocean before: between 1953 and 1960 they appeared regularly in the New York Times "Review of the Week." Currently Schoenfeld cartoons are published in Germany in the *Hamburger Abendblatt, Tagesspiegel* (Berlin), *Neue Ruhr Zeitung* (Essen) and *Rheinpfalz* (Ludwigshafen).

But Schoenfeld's first love is painting, and he is finding more time now to return to it. His style, which comes from his studies, is expressionism. Perhaps some day this work too will come to the United States!

Hans Stenzel (Zel) was born in the United States, in Louisville, in 1923. His family had fled the devastating inflation that swept Germany in the years following World War I; but in the U.S. they found themselves denied their favorite beverages by the Prohibition laws then in effect, and returned to Germany.

Stenzel believes his abilities were inherited from his mother's happy disposition and his father's artistic talent as a painter. These abilities produced a prodigious output—Stenzel estimates he has published 165,000 drawings—which has earned him wide recognition, including the "Golden Palm" first prize in Italy's Bordighera "Salone internazionale dell Umorismo."

Stenzel served as a medical orderly in the Second World War and commemorated his experiences in a sardonic novel entitled *Three Cheers.*

Lothar Ursinus was the son of parents impoverished during the First World War. He was orphaned while still a child.

He began to draw at an early age, and was able to study at the "Graphische Akademie" in Leipzig. With the beginning of World War II he was recruited as an ordinary soldier and became a prisoner of war in 1944. This led to internment in

England and then in Canada. He was finally released in East
Germany, but left as quickly as possible, finding refuge with
a friend in Kiel (West Germany).

During the War he produced a diary of drawings, but in Kiel
he first found work as an advertising agent. Soon, however,
he began to sell his cartoons, and was finally able to support
himself as a cartoonist. For many years now he has been a
contributor to both German and Swiss publications.

Ursinus still lives in Kiel, where he is married and has three
children. He still finds great enjoyment in his work.

Grosse

„Tierversuche?—Nein, das machen wir nicht!"

Key Words

Tierversuche	animal experiments
machen (*v., inf.*)	do

Everyday English

"Experiment with animals? No, we don't do that."

Grosse

„Dies ist der erste Virus den Sie mit blossem Auge entdecken können Herr Kollege."

Key Words

können	to be able to, can
erste (*adj.*)	first
blossem (bloss, *adj.*)	bare, naked
Auge (*n., n.*)	eye
entdecken (*v., inf.*)	detect, discover
Kollege (*n., m.*)	colleague

Everyday English

"This is the first virus that you can detect with the naked eye, Professor."

Grosse

„10 Vaterunser dürften vorerst genügen . . ."

Key Words

Vaterunser (*n.*, *n.*)	The Lord's Prayer
dürften (*v.*, dürfen *inf.*)	should
vorerst	for the time being
genügen (*v.*, *inf.*)	to suffice
Rezepte (*n.*, *n.*, *pl.*)	prescriptions

Everyday English

"Ten prayers a day should do it for now."

Grosse

„Sie müssen wissen, mein Herr, normalerweise flieg' ich selbst."

Key Words

müssen (*v., inf.*)	must
wissen (*v., inf.*)	know
normalerweise (*adv.*)	normally
flieg' (fliege, *v.*, fliegen *inf.*)	fly
selbst (*pron.*)	self

Everyday English

"I'd like you to know, sir, that normally I fly myself."

Grosse

„Immer schön eins nach dem Andern."

Key Words

immer (*adv.*)	always
schön (*adj.*)	nicely
Andern (ander)	other

Everyday English

"Let's just do one thing at a time."

Grosse

„Selbstverständlich sind Sie nicht mein erster prominenter Patient."

Key Words

selbstverständlich (*adv.*)	obviously
erster	first
prominenter (prominent, *adj.*)	prominent

Everyday English

"Obviously, you are not my first prominent patient."

„Die nächste Gruppe bitte."

Key Words

heute	today
Gruppen-Therapie (*n., f.*)	group therapy
nächste (*adj.*)	next
Gruppe (*n., f.*)	group

Everyday English

Group Therapy Today
"The next group please."

Grosse

„Ich brauch' nähere Angaben! Name, Geburtsdatum, u.s.w."

Key Words

Geburtsdatum	date of birth
brauch' (brauche, *v.*, brauchen *inf.*)	need
nähere (*adj., pl.*)	further
Angaben (*n., f., pl.*)	data
u.s.w. (und so weiter)	et cetera

Everyday English

"I need more precise data: name, date of birth, etc."

Grosse

„Stimmt's, Sie sind der Unsichtbare?!"

Key Words

stimmt's (*v.*, stimmen *inf.*)   be correct
Unsichtbare (*n., m.*)   invisible man

Everyday English

"You are the invisible man, yes?"

Grosse

„Warum können Sie denn nicht Napoleon, Lincoln oder Socrates sein? Wie alle Anderen auch?!"

Key Words

können (*v., inf.*)	to be able to
wie (*conj.*)	like
alle (*adj.*)	all
Anderen (*n., pl.*)	others

Everyday English

"Why can't you be Napoleon, Lincoln or Socrates like everybody else?"

Grosse

Key Words

Hund (*n., m.*)	dog
runter (*adv.*)	down
vom (von dem)	from

Everyday English

"Dog?"

"Yes, I am a dog."

"Ugh! Get off the couch!"

Grosse

„Er meint er ist Superman!!"
„Kommen Sie, liebe Frau, wir klären ihn unten auf."

Key Words

meint (*v.*, meinen *inf.*)	imagine
kommen (*v.*, *inf.*)	come
liebe (*adj.*)	dear
Frau (*n.*, *f.*)	madam
klären ... auf (*v.*, aufklären *inf.*)	enlighten
unten (*adv.*)	downstairs

Everyday English

Wife: "He thinks he's Superman!"
Doctor: "Come, dear lady, we'll explain it to him downstairs."

Grosse

„Verzeihung Herr Amtsrat, ich kann nicht schreiben, ich bin Analphabet."
„Ach das macht nichts, ich bin Diabetiker."

Key Words

Verzeihung (*n., f.*)	excuse me
Amtsrat (*n., m.*)	officer
kann (*v., können inf.*)	to be able to
schreiben (*v., inf.*)	write
Analphabet (*n., m.*)	illiterate
ach	oh
macht (*v., machen inf.*)	make
nichts	nothing
Diabetiker	diabetic

Everyday English

"Excuse me, sir, I can't write, I am illiterate."
"No problem. I am diabetic."

Grosse

„Was haben die nur gegen uns Beamte.—Wir tun doch nichts!"

Key Words

nur	only
gegen (*prep.*)	against
Beamte (Beamter, *n., m., pl.*)	bureaucrat
tun (*v., inf.*)	to do
nichts	nothing

Everyday English

"What do they have against us bureaucrats? After all, we don't do anything."

Grosse

„So Herbert, bis zur Pensionierung halten wir noch leicht durch! Gell?"

Key Words

bis	until
zur (zu der)	to the
Pensionierung (*n., f.*)	retirement
halten ... durch (*v.,* durchhalten *inf.*)	hold on, stick it out
leicht (*adv.*)	easily
gell? (*colloq.*)	isn't it so?

Everyday English

"So, Herbert, we'll stick it out easily till retirement, won't we?"

Grosse

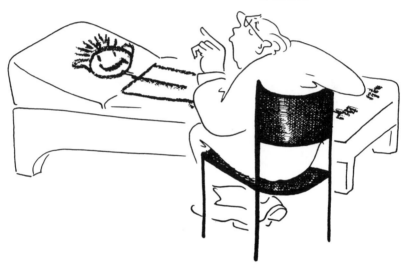

„Seit wann, Herr Hitz, glauben Sie denn Linienpilot zu sein?"

Key Words

Prüfer (*n., m.*)	examiner
Kl. (Klasse)	class
seit (*prep.*)	since
wann	when
glauben (*v., inf.*)	believe
Linienpilot	airline pilot

Everyday English

"Since when have you believed you were an airLINE pilot, Herr Hitz?"

Grosse

„Ich habe grosse Angst, sehr, sehr jung zu sterben."
„Aber, aber—Davor brauchen Sie doch jetzt keine Angst mehr zu haben."

Key Words

grosse (gross, *adj.*)	great
Angst (*n., f.*)	fear
sehr (*adv.*)	very
jung (*adj.*)	young
sterben (*v., inf.*)	die
davor	of that
brauchen (*v., inf.*)	need
jetzt	now
mehr	more

Everyday English

"I have this terrible fear of dying very young."
"Well, well, you don't have to worry about THAT any more."

Grosse

Grosse

„Was haben Sie denn ganz am Anfang gemacht?"
„Oh, am Anfang schuf ich Himmel und Erde."

Key Words

ganz (*adv.*)	entirely
Anfang (*n., m.*)	beginning
gemacht (*v.*, machen *inf.*)	do
schuf (*v.*, schaffen *inf.*)	create
Himmel (*n., m.*)	sky, heaven
Erde (*n., f.*)	earth

Everyday English

"What did you do in the beginning?"
"Oh, in the beginning I created heaven and earth."

Langer

Key Words

trinken (*v., inf.*)   drink

mässig (*adv.*)   moderately

Everyday English

"You drink?"

"Moderately."

Key Words

wird (*v.*, werden *inf.*)	will
gut (*adj.*)	good
tun (*v., inf.*)	to do

Everyday English

"This will do you good."

Key Words

entschuldigen	excuse (me)
verstehe (*v.,* verstehen *inf.*)	understand

Everyday English

"Excuse me, but I understand only I.B.M."

Langer

„Ich rauche nicht. Ich trinke nicht. Ich esse vernünftig. Ich treibe Sport. Vermeide Stress, ergibt eine Lebenserwartung von . . . ENORM!! Aber was fange ich mit der vielen Zeit an?"

Key Words

rauche (*v.*, rauchen *inf.*)	smoke
trinke (*v.*, trinken *inf.*)	drink
esse (*v.*, essen *inf.*)	eat
vernünftig (*adv.*)	reasonably
treibe (*v.*, treiben *inf.*)	(in this sense) practice, do
vermeide (*v.*, vermeiden *inf.*)	avoid
ergibt (*v.*, ergeben *inf.*)	result in
Lebenserwartung (*n.*, *f.*)	life expectancy
fange . . . an (*v.*, anfangen *inf.*)	begin, to do (with)
vielen (viel, *adj.*)	much
Zeit (*n.*, *f.*)	time

Everyday English

"I don't smoke. I don't drink. I eat reasonably. I go in for sports. I avoid stress, and my life expectancy is . . . ENORMOUS. But what will I do with this much time?"

Key Words

esst (*v., essen inf.*)	eat
mehr (*adj.*)	more
Rindfleisch (*n., n.*)	beef

Everyday English

"Eat more beef."

Diese Wiese widmet Ihnen VITAL Haarwuchs Mittel

Key Words

Wiese (*n.*, *f.*)	meadow
widmet (*v.*, widmen *inf.*)	sponsored by
Haarwuchs (Haar + wuchs)	hair-growing
Mittel (*n.*, *n.*)	remedy

Everyday English

"This meadow is sponsored by VITAL Cure for Baldness."

Langer

„Für einen Hungerkünstler sehen Sie ziemlich gut aus."

Key Words

Hungerkünstler (*n., m.*)	starving artist
sehen . . . aus (*v., inf.*)	look
gut (*adj.*)	good
ziemlich (*adv.*)	rather

Everyday English

"For a starving artist, you look pretty good."

Möllendorff

„Habe ich nun die anderen Bilder auch verkehrt rum aufgehängt?"

Key Words

anderen (ander, *adj.*)	other
Bilder (*n., n., pl.*)	pictures
verkehrt rum	upside down
aufgehängt (*v.,* aufhängen *inf.*)	hang up

Everyday English

"Now, did I hang the other pictures upside down as well?"

Möllendorff

MÖLLENDORFF

„Erschrecken Sie nicht, diesen Rat habe ich mir von dem neuen Berliner Hundepsychologen geholt, mein Fiffi wollte keinen Maulkorb tragen."

Key Words

erschrecken (*v., inf.*)	frighten
Rat (*n., m.*)	advice
neuen (neu, *adj.*)	new
Hundepsychologen (*n., m.*)	dog psychologist
geholt (*v.,* holen *inf.*)	get from
wollte (*v.,* wollen *inf.*)	want
keinen (kein)	not any
Maulkorb (*n., m.*)	muzzle
tragen (*v., inf.*)	wear

Everyday English

"Don't be scared—the new Berlin dog psychologist gave me this advice when Fiffi did not want to wear a muzzle."

Möllendorff

„Ja, ja, ich warte, Fiffi, ich weiss ja, dein Frauchen hat wieder den modernen engen Rock an."

Key Words

warte (*v.,* warten *inf.*)	wait
weiss (*v.,* wissen *inf.*)	know
Frauchen (*dim. of* Frau)	little woman
hat . . . an (*v.,* anhaben *inf.*)	wear
wieder (*adv.*)	again
modernen (modern, *adj.*)	modern, stylish
engen (eng, *adj.*)	narrow
Rock (*n., m.*)	skirt

Everyday English

"Yes, Fiffi, I'll wait—I know your mistress is wearing her stylish narrow skirt again."

Möllendorff

„Ich finde das nicht witzig!"
„Ich ja, du sitzt lieber im Schatten und ich in der Sonne."

Key Words

finde (*v.*, finden *inf.*)	find
witzig (*adj.*)	funny
sitzt (*v.*, sitzen *inf.*)	sit
lieber (*adv.*)	rather
Schatten (*n., m.*)	shade
Sonne (*n., f.*)	sun

Everyday English

"That's not funny."
"Yes, it is. You prefer the shade and I like the sun."

Möllendorff

„Bei Ihrem vorigen Gastspiel müssen die ja einen Ärger gehabt
haben!"
„Ärger haben die nicht gehabt, die sind in einen
Begeisterungssturm geraten."

Key Words

vorigen (vorig, *adj.*)	previous
Gastspiel (*n., n.*)	performance
müssen (*v., inf.*)	must
Ärger (*n., m.*)	anger
Begeisterungssturm (*n., m.*)	storm of enthusiasm
geraten (*v., inf.*)	get into

Everyday English

"They must have had a rough time at their last performance."
"It wasn't that; at their last performance they met with a
storm of enthusiasm."

Möllendorff

„Hallo, wenn Sie uns noch länger ärgern, kommen wir runter! Hören Sie endlich auf, Ihre Braut gegen unsere Klingelknöpfe zu drücken!"

Key Words

hallo	hello
länger (*adv.*)	longer
ärgern (*v., inf.*)	anger, to make cross
kommen (*v., inf.*)	come
runter (*adv.*)	down
hören . . . auf (*v.,* aufhören *inf.*)	stop
endlich (*adv.*)	at last
Braut (*n., f.*)	fiancee
gegen (*adv.*)	against
Klingelknöpfe (*n., m., pl.*)	doorbells
drücken (*v., inf.*)	press

Everyday English

"Hey there, if you keep annoying us we'll come down. Stop leaning your fiancee against the doorbells!"

Möllendorff

„Jahrelang hat sich keiner um mich gekümmert, wenn ich jetzt aus dem Fenster kucke ist Jubel, Trubel, Heiterkeit."

Key Words

jahrelang (*adv.*)	for years
keiner	no one
gekümmert (*v.*, kümmern *inf.*)	take notice of
wenn	when
jetzt (*adv.*)	now
Fenster (*n., m.*)	window
kucke (*colloq. for v.*, gucken *inf.*)	look
Jubel (*n., m.*)	jubilation, rejoicing
Trubel (*n., m.*)	excitement
Heiterkeit (*n., n.*)	hilarity

Everyday English

"For years nobody noticed me. Now when I look out the window there's laughter and excitement."

Möllendorff

„Ach, jetzt hat er nach dem langen Winterschlaf auch noch die Frühjahrsmüdigkeit."

Key Words

ach (*exclam.*)	alas
jetzt (*adv.*)	now
langen (lang, *adj.*)	long
Winterschlaf (*n., m.*)	hibernation
Frühjahrsmüdigkeit (*n., f.*)	spring fever

Everyday English

"Alas, after his long hibernation, now he has spring fever."

Möllendorff

„Guter Weihnachtsmann, hast du schon überall kräftig mitgefeiert?"
„Wie kommt Ihr darauf?"
„Du hast die Maske verkehrt herum auf!"

Key Words

guter (gut, *adj.*)	good
Weihnachtsmann (*n., m.*)	Santa Claus
schon (*adv.*)	already
überall (*adv.*)	everywhere
kräftig (*adj.*)	strong(ly)
mitgefeiert (*v.,* mitfeiern *inf.*)	participate in a celebration
kommt (*v.,* kommen *inf.*)	come
darauf (*adv.*)	upon that
Maske (*n., f.*)	mask
verkehrt (*adv.*)	reverse
hast . . . auf (*v.,* aufhaben *inf.*)	wear

Everyday English

"Dear Santa Claus, have you participated in all the festivities?"
"Why do you ask?"
"Your mask is upside down!"

Schoenfeld

Key Words

Gebühren (*n., f., pl.*)	fees
Bezirksamt (*n., n.*)	district office
Herein	come in
sagen (*v., inf.*)	say
Guten Tag	good day, hello
wünschen (*v., inf.*)	want
Stempel (*n., m.*)	rubber stamp
anfeuchten (*v., inf.*)	dampen
stempeln (*v., inf.*)	to stamp (something)
Auf Wiedersehen	good-bye

Everyday English

Fees

To say "Come in"	−.20	
To say "Hello"	−.20	District Office
To say "What do you want?"	−.40	
To ink the rubber stamp	−.50	
To stamp something	1.−	
To say "Good-bye"	−.70	
TOTAL DM	3. −	

Schoenfeld

„Streiken dürfen wir nicht, auf Gehaltserhöhung sollen wir verzichten, und nun müssen wir auch noch hilfsbereit sein!"

Key Words

Sachbearbeiter (*n., m.*)	caseworker
Anmeldungen (*n., f., pl.*)	registrations
Abmeld. (Abmeldungen) (*n., f., pl.*)	departure notices
Ummeldungen (*n., f., pl.*)	moving notices
Anträge (*n., m., pl.*)	applications
streiken (*v., inf.*)	strike
dürfen (*v., inf.*)	to be allowed to
Gehaltserhöhung (*n., f.*)	raise (in salary)
sollen (*v., inf.*)	must
verzichten (*v., inf.*)	to do without
müssen (*v., inf.*)	must
hilfsbereit (*adj.*)	helpful

Everyday English

Door: Applications A–D
Sign: Registration for Departure and Moving Notices
Desk: Caseworker
"We can't strike, we must do without a raise, and now, in addition, we are expected to be helpful!"

Schoenfeld

„Melde gehorsamst: Noch 11 Gefangene gemacht!"

Key Words

melde (*v.*, melden *inf.*)	report
gehorsamst (*adv.*)	obediently
Gefangene (*n.*, *m.*, *pl.*)	prisoners
gemacht (*v.*, machen *inf.*)	take

Everyday English

"Sir! I wish to report: eleven more prisoners taken."

Schoenfeld

Schlaftablette der Neuzeit
„Wer hat mein Schlafmittel ausgemacht?"

Key Words

Schlafmittel (*n., n.*)	sleeping pill
ausgemacht (*v., ausmachen inf.*)	switch off
Neuzeit (*n., f.*)	modern times
Schlaftablette (*n., n., pl.*)	sleeping pills

Everyday English

Sleeping pills for today.
"Who turned off my sleeping pill?"

Key Words

hier (*adv.*)	here
spricht (*v.*, sprechen *inf.*)	speak
Arzt (*n., m.*)	doctor
werfen ... ein (*v.*, einwerfen *inf.*)	throw in
Krankenschein (*n., m.*)	medical report
schildern (*v., inf.*)	describe
Beschwerden (*n., f., pl.*)	complaints
Praxis (*n., f.*)	practice
Sprechstunde (*n., f.*)	consultation hours
Rezepte (*n., n., pl.*)	prescriptions
entnehmen (*v., inf.*)	take out

Everyday English

"This is the doctor speaking. Deposit your medical report and describe your symptoms."
Practice of Dr. Knox.
Consultation hours 9–11 a.m. and 5–7 p.m.
Take out your prescription here.

Schoenfeld

„Das Haus habt ihr verkauft, damit wir studieren können—O.K., aber was wollt ihr uns mal vererben?"

Key Words

Haus (*n.*, *n.*)	house
verkauft (*v.*, verkaufen *inf.*)	sell
damit (*conj.*)	so that
studieren (*v.*, *inf.*)	study
können (*v.*, *inf.*)	can
wollt (*v.*, wollen *inf.*)	will
vererben (*v.*, *inf.*)	leave (to heirs)

Everyday English

"You've sold the house so that we can go to the university—O.K., but what will you leave us when the time comes?"

Zel

„Endlich schönes Wetter . . ."

Key Words

Kohlen (*n., f., pl.*)	coal
Heizöl (*n., n.*)	heating oil
endlich (*adv.*)	at last
schönes (schön, *adj.*)	beautiful
Wetter (*n., n.*)	weather

Everyday English

Proprietor of coal store to proprietor of heating oil store: "At last, beautiful weather!"

Zel

„Typisch . . . Wo schon was ist kommt noch was zu!"

Key Words

Elektrizitätswerk (*n., n.*)	power plant
typisch (*adj.*)	typical
schon (*adv.*)	already
kommt . . . zu (*v.*, hinzukommen *inf.*)	be added to
was (etwas, *pron.*)	something

Everyday English

"Typical . . . them that has, gets!"

„Lass die Scherze, Karl-Hermann . . ."

Key Words

lass (*v.*, lassen *inf.*)   stop
Scherze (*n., m., pl.*)   nonsense, jokes

Everyday English

"Stop that nonsense, Karl-Hermann!"

Zel

Wachhund
Wegen Betriebsferien bitte selber bellen!

Key Words

wegen (*conj.*)	because of
Betriebsferien (*n., f.*)	vacation
selber (*pron.*)	self
bellen (*v., inf.*)	bark
Wachhund (*n., m.*)	watchdog

Everyday English

Watchdog. Closed for vacation. Please do your own barking.

Zel

Ostern auf dem Truppenübungsplatz

Key Words

Ostern (*n., n.*)	Easter
Truppenübungsplatz (*n., m.*)	army drill ground

Everyday English

Easter on the army drill ground

Zel

„Genau wie Du: Immer die Hand auf der Brieftasche!"

Key Words

genau (*adv.*)	exactly
wie (*prep.*)	like
immer (*adv.*)	always
Brieftasche (*n., f.*)	wallet

Everyday English

"Just like you. Always the hand on the wallet."

Zel

"Der Einzige, der keinen Raucherhusten bekommt!"

Key Words

Einzige (*n., m.*)	only one
keinen (*adj.*)	no, not any
Raucherhusten (*n., m.*)	smoker's cough
bekommt (*v.,* bekommen *inf.*)	get
Vesuv	Mount Vesuvius

Everyday English

"That's the only one that doesn't get a smoker's cough!"

Zel

Auch der Herbst hat schöne Tage . . .

Key Words

Herbst (*n., m.*)	autumn
schöne (schön, *adj.*)	beautiful
Tage (*n., m., pl.*)	days

Everyday English

Even autumn has its beautiful days . . .

Zel

Donnerstags bis 21 Uhr geöffnet!

Key Words

Donnerstags (*n., m.*)	Thursdays
bis (*prep.*)	until
Uhr (*n., f.*)	hour
geöffnet (*v.,* öffnen *inf.*)	open

Everyday English

Open Thursdays until 9 p.m.

Zel

„Warten Sie schon lange?"

Key Words

Wartezimmer (*n., n.*)	waiting room
warten (*v., inf.*)	wait
lange (*adv.*)	long time

Everyday English

Sign: Waiting room.
"Have you been waiting long?"

Zel

„Bitte, ein Einzelzimmer mit sieben Kinderbetten . . ."

Key Words

Einzelzimmer (*n., n.*)	single room
sieben	seven
Kinderbetten (*n., n., pl.*)	children's beds
Schneewittchen	Snow White

Everyday English

Snow White: "A single room with seven cots, please."

„In diesem Sonderbus können Sie unser Sauwetter zweistöckig sehen . . .“

Key Words

Sonderbus (*n., m.*)	special bus
können (*v., inf.*)	be able to
Sauwetter (*n., n.*)	foul weather
zweistöckig	double decker
sehen (*v., inf.*)	see

Everyday English

“On this special bus, our foul weather can be seen from both levels.”

Zel

„Na? Trägt das Eis?"

Key Words

trägt (*v.*, tragen *inf.*)	carry
Eis (*n.*, *n.*)	ice

Everyday English

"Well? Does the ice hold?"

Zel

„Stör'n se nich die Amtshandlung eines Strafzettelschreibers . . .“

Key Words

stör'n (*v.,* stören *inf.*)	disturb
nich (nicht)	not
Amtshandlung (*n., f.*)	official act
Strafzettelschreibers	writer of traffic tickets
(Strafzettelschreiber,	(fine + writer)
n., m.)	

Everyday English

"Do not interrupt an officer in the act of writing a parking ticket."

Zel

„Nichts zu machen: se streiken!"

Key Words

machen (*v., inf.*)	to do
streiken (*v., inf.*)	to be on strike
Fluchtauto (*n., n.*)	getaway car

Everyday English

"Nothing doing. They're on strike!"

Key Words

Krankenhaus (*n., n.*)   hospital
fehlt (*v.,* fehlen *inf.*)   lack, be wrong with

Everyday English

At the hospital: "What are you suffering from?"
"A doctor."

Zel

Der ideale Kellner

Key Words

ideal (*adj.*)	ideal
Kellner (*n., m.*)	waiter

Everyday English

The ideal waiter

Zel

Stoppt Tiefflüge

Key Words

stoppt (*v.*, stoppen *inf.*)   stop
Tiefflüge (Tiefflug, *n.*, *m.*, *pl.*)   low flights

Everyday English

Stop low flights

Zel

„Freitag, der 13.? Alles Blödsinn!"

Key Words

Freitag (*n., m.*)   Friday
alles (*pron.*)   everything
Blödsinn (*n., m.*)   nonsense

Everyday English

"Friday the Thirteenth? That's all nonsense!"

Zel

Hitzewelle

Key Words

tausche (*v.,* tauschen *inf.*)	exchange
Bärenfell (*n., m.*)	bearskin
gegen (*prep.*)	against
Badehose (*n., f.*)	bathing suit
Hitzewelle (*n., f.*)	heat wave
Grönland	Greenland

Everyday English

Heat wave—Greenland
Sign: Will exchange bearskin for swim trunks!

Zel

„Keene Angst—ich rauche draussen!"

Key Words

Nichtraucher (*n., m.*)	nonsmoker
keene (*colloq. for* keine)	no
Angst (*n., f.*)	fear
rauche (*v.*, rauchen *inf.*)	to smoke
draussen (*adv.*)	outside

Everyday English

No-Smoking Taxi
"Don't worry—I'm smoking outside!"

Zel

„Pass auf dass Du nicht auf ein U-Boot springst!"

Key Words

pass auf (*v.,* aufpassen *inf.*)	take care
dass (*conj.*)	that
U-Boot (*n., m.*)	submarine
springst (*v.,* springen *inf.*)	jump, dive

Everyday English

"Careful, don't dive onto a submarine!"

James Bond war hier.

Key Words

hier (*adv.*)   here

Everyday English

James Bond was here.

Zel

„Wird Zeit, dass du Winter-Reifen rauf machst . . ."

Key Words

wird (*v.,* werden *inf.*)	become
Zeit (*n., f.*)	time
dass (*conj.*)	that
Winter-Reifen (*n., m., pl.*)	snow tires
rauf (*colloq. for* darauf, drauf)	on it
machst (*v.,* machen *inf.*)	make, do

Everyday English

"It's about time you changed to snow tires . . ."

Zel

„Habt Ihr auch keinen Führerschein mehr?"

Key Words

habt (*v.*, haben *inf.*)	have
keinen (*adj.*)	no
Führerschein (*n., m.*)	driver's license
mehr (*adv.*)	more
gehen (*v., inf.*)	go, walk, jog

Everyday English

50 Kilometer Walk
"Have they taken away your driver's license too?"

Zel

„Wat für eine Ausbildung braucht man, wenn man Playboy werden will?"

Key Words

Berufsberatung (*n., f.*)	job counseling
wat (*colloq. for* was, *pron.*)	what
was für ein	what kind of
Ausbildung (*n., f.*)	training, studies
braucht (*v.,* brauchen *inf.*)	need
man	one
werden (*v., inf.*)	become
will (*v.,* wollen *inf.*)	want to

Everyday English

Job Counseling

"What does one have to study to become a playboy?"

Zel

Altbau-Modernisierung

Key Words

Altbau (*n., m.*)   old housing
Modernisierung (*n., f.*)   modernization

Everyday English

Modernization of old housing

Zel

„. . . aber in's Meer schüttet Ihr es umsonst!"

Key Words

Benzin (*n., n.*)	gasoline
teurer (*adv.*)	higher, more expensive
in's (*colloq., in das*)	into the
Meer (*n., n.*)	sea
schüttet (*v.,* schütten *inf.*)	pour
umsonst (*adv.*)	free of charge

Everyday English

Gasoline price up!

". . . but you pour it into the ocean for free!"

Zel

„Endstation! Alles aussteigen!"

Key Words

Endstation (*n., f.*)	terminal
alles (*adj., colloq. for* alle)	everybody, all
aussteigen (*v., inf.*)	get out, disembark

Everyday English

"Last stop! Everybody out!"

Zel

„. . . umweltfreundlich: mit Schalldämpfer . . ."

Key Words

Everyday English

Night flights prohibited
". . . environmentally friendly: with silencer . . ."

Zel

Tennis-Unterricht

Key Words

Unterricht (*n., m.*)   lesson

Everyday English

Tennis lesson

Zel

„Wie Marlene Dietrich—bloss kürzere Beine . . .“

Key Words

Dackel (*n., m.*)	Dachshund
Schönheits-Wettbewerb (*n., m.*)	beauty contest
wie	as, like
bloss (*adv.*)	only
kürzere (*adj.*)	shorter
Beine (*n., n., pl.*)	legs

Everyday English

Dachshund Beauty Contest

"Just like Marlene Dietrich—only the legs are shorter..."

Zel

„Willst wohl mal Finanzminister werden?"

Key Words

willst (*v.*, wollen *inf.*)	want to
wohl (*adv.*)	well
mal (*adv., colloq. for* einmal)	some day (in the future)
Finanzminister	finance minister
werden (*v., inf.*)	become

Everyday English

"You've figured out the best way to become finance minister some day."

Zel

„Bisschen viel Tennis gesehen, nicht wahr?"

Key Words

bisschen (*adv.*)	a bit
viel (*adv.*)	much
gesehen (*v.*, sehen *inf.*)	see, watch
wahr (*adj.*)	true, real

Everyday English

"You've been watching a bit too much tennis, wouldn't you say?"

Zel

"Sogar die Fische klappern mit den Zähnen."

Key Words

sogar (*adv.*)	even
Fische (*n., m., pl.*)	fish
klappern (*v., inf.*)	chatter
Zähnen (*n., m., pl.*)	teeth

Everyday English

"Even the fish's teeth are chattering..."

Zel

„Wasserflöhe? Zählen Sie mal selber nach . . .“

Key Words

Tierzählung (*n., f.*)	animal census
Wasserflöhe (*n., m., pl.*)	waterfleas
zählen . . . nach (*v.,* nachzählen *inf.*)	count
selber (*pron.*)	self, yourself

Everyday English

Animal census

“Waterfleas? Why don't you count them yourself...”

Ursinus

Immer mehr wird die Krankenschwester zur unverzichtbaren Stütze des Arztes.

Key Words

immer (*adv.*)	always
mehr (*adv.*)	more
wird (*v.,* werden *inf.*)	become
Krankenschwester (*n., f.*)	nurse
zur (zu der)	into
unverzichtbaren (unverzichtbar, *adj.*)	indispensable
Stütze (*n., f.*)	support
Arztes (Arzt, *n., m.*)	doctor

Everyday English

More and more the nurse has become the doctor's indispensable support.

„Sie sind nicht der richtige Typ Mensch für den Kauf eines solchen Wagens."

Key Words

richtige (richtig, *adj.*)	correct, right
Typ (*n., m.*)	type
Mensch (*n., m.*)	man, human being
Kauf (*n., m.*)	purchase
solchen (solch, *adj.*)	such
Wagens (Wagen, *n., m.*)	car

Everyday English

"You're not the right type of person for this car."

Ursinus

„Herr Tschang wird Ihnen die Speisekarte übersetzen."

Key Words

Speisekarte (*n., f.*) menu
übersetzen (*v., inf.*) translate

Everyday English

"Mr. Chang will translate the menu for you."

Ursinus

Trinkgeld nach Belieben

Key Words

Trinkgeld (*n., n.*)   tip
Belieben (*n., n.*)   choice

Everyday English

"Tip at your discretion."

Ursinus

„Ehrlich! Zu zweit zahlen sich Autoschulden viel leichter."

Key Words

ehrlich (*adv.*)	honestly
zu zweit	as a twosome, two people
zahlen (*v., inf.*)	pay
Autoschulden (*n., f., pl.*)	car payments
viel (*adv.*)	much
leichter (leicht, *adv.*)	easier

Everyday English

"To tell the truth, it's much easier for two people to handle the car payments."

Ursinus

„Es war bei Ihnen ein ganz reizender Abend."

Key Words

bei Ihnen   with you, at your house

ganz (*adv.*)   very

reizender (reizend, *adj.*)   charming, very nice

Abend (*n., m.*)   evening

Everyday English

"It was a very lovely evening at your place."

Ane

„Schon gehört? Blutkonserven werden knapp. Lass uns noch schnell den Dicken da anzapfen!"

Key Words

gehört (v., hören inf.)	hear
Blutkonserven (n., f., pl.)	blood reserves
werden (aux. v.)	become
knapp (adv.)	scarce
lass (v., lassen inf.)	let
schnell (adv.)	quickly
Dicken (Dicker, n., m.)	the fat one
anzapfen (v., inf.)	tap

Everyday English

"Have you heard? Blood reserves are down. Let's tap the big one over there right away."

Ane

„Frühjahrsmüdigkeit trifft ganz besonders Beamte.—Weil sie kein bewegliches Ziel sind . . .“

Key Words

Frühjahrsmüdigkeit (*n., f.*)	spring fever
trifft (*v.*, treffen *inf.*)	hit
ganz (*adv.*)	entirely
besonders (*adv.*)	particularly
Beamte (Beamter, *n., m., pl.*)	bureaucrats
weil (*conj.*)	because
bewegliches (beweglich, *adj.*)	movable
Ziel (*n., m.*)	target

Everyday English

"Spring fever hits bureaucrats easily because they are not moving targets."

Ane

„Herr Parkwächter, dieser Lümmel da hat mich tätlich angegriffen!"

Key Words

Herr (*n., m.*)	Mr.
Parkwächter (*n., m.*)	park guardian
Lümmel (*n., m.*)	lout
tätlich (*adv.*)	violently
angegriffen (*v.,* angreifen *inf.*)	attack

Everyday English

"Officer, this rascal has violently wounded me."

Ane

„Sag mal, Schwesterherz, du weisst doch schon wie's lang geht. Was schenkt man denn so zum Muttertag?"

Key Words

Schwesterherz	sister dear
sag (*v.,* sagen *inf.*)	say
weisst (*v.,* wissen *inf.*)	know
wie's (wie es, *adv.*)	how
lang (*adv.*)	along
geht (*v.,* gehen *inf.*)	go
wissen wie's lang geht (*colloq.*)	to know the ropes
schenkt (*v.,* schenken *inf.*)	give
man (*pron.*)	one
zum (zu dem, *prep.*)	for
Muttertag (*n., m.*)	Mother's Day

Everyday English

"Tell me, sister darling, you know the ropes. What does one give for Mother's Day?"

Ane

„Was denn, Heiligabend zieh'n sie auch 'ne Show ab?! Sind Sie nicht der Typ, der wochenlang in zig Kaufhäusern aufgetreten ist?"

Key Words

Heiligabend (*n., m.*)	Christmas Eve
zieh'n ... ab (*v., colloq.* abziehen *inf.*)	put on (a show)
'ne (eine, *colloq.*)	a, one
Typ (*n., m.*)	guy, person
wochenlang (*adv.*)	for weeks
zig (*colloq.*)	several
Kaufhäusern (*n., n., pl.*)	department stores
aufgetreten (*v.,* auftreten *inf.*)	appear, perform

Everyday English

"What's this, you're turning up again on Christmas Eve? Aren't you the guy who's been in all the department stores for the last couple of weeks?"

Ane

„Au Mann, ist der Frass mal wieder lasch! Seitdem du zu den Baumschützern gehörst—hast du generell was gegen Salz, oder?"

Key Words

Mann (*n., m.*)	man
Frass (*colloq., n., m.*)	food (mostly for animals)
wieder (*adv.*)	again
lasch (*adj.*)	tasteless
seitdem (*conj.*)	since
Baumschützern (Baumschützer, *n., m., pl.*)	tree protectors (environmentalists)
gehörst (*v.,* gehören *inf.*)	belong
generell (*adv.*)	generally, on principle
gegen (*prep.*)	against
Salz (*n., n.*)	salt

Everyday English

"Oh man, is this grub tasteless! Ever since you joined the environmental group you're against salt on principle, eh?"

Ane

„Also, im Sucher ist kein Elefant zu sehen. Steig herunter, was Du geschossen hast, war 'ne Fata Morgana."

Key Words

also (*adv.*)	so
im (*prep.*)	in the
Sucher (*n., m.*)	viewfinder
Elefant (*n., m.*)	elephant
sehen (*v., inf.*)	see
steig (*v.,* steigen *inf.*)	climb
herunter (*adv.*)	down
geschossen (*v.,* schiessen *inf.*)	shot
'ne (eine)	a
Fata Morgana (*n., f.*)	mirage

Everyday English

"Come down to earth—there's no elephant in the viewfinder. You shot a mirage."

Ane

„—und ich war der Meinung, Sieger beim Riesenslalom wird der, der das meiste Holz zusammenbringt."

Key Words

Ziel (*n., n.*)	finish line
Meinung (*n., f.*)	opinion
Sieger (*n., m.*)	winner
Riesenslalom (*n., m.*)	giant slalom
wird (*v.,* werden *inf.*)	become
meiste (meist, *adj.*)	most
Holz (*n., n.*)	(in this sense) flag
zusammenbringt (*v.,* zusammenbringen *inf.*)	collect

Everyday English

At the finish line: "... and I thought the winner of the giant slalom was the one who collected the most flags!"

Ane

„Junger Mann, Sie haben vielleicht Humor; ausgerechnet am 1. April mit ernsten Absichten zu kommen."

Key Words

junger (jung, *adj.*)	young
Mann (*n., m.*)	man
vielleicht (*adv.*)	perhaps
Humor (*n., m.*)	(sense of) humor
ausgerechnet (*adv.*)	exactly when
ernsten (ernst, *adj.*)	serious
Absichten (*n., f., pl.*)	intentions
kommen (*v., inf.*)	come

Everyday English

"Young man, you have a real sense of humor to come precisely on April first with serious intentions."

Ane

„Jetzt unsere super neue Kopfschmerz-Tablette genommen—und Sie fühlen sich wie vorher."

Key Words

jetzt (*adv.*)	now
neue (*adj.*)	new
Kopfschmerz (*n., m.*)	headache
Tablette (*n., f., pl.*)	pills
genommen (*v.*, nehmen *inf.*)	take
fühlen (*v., inf.*)	feel
wie (*conj.*)	as, like
vorher (*adv.*)	before

Everyday English

"Now if you will take our new super headache pill, you'll feel like new!"

Ane

„Na, wollen wir dem Opa auch noch einen Schuss Lebensfreude vermitteln?"

Key Words

wollen (*v., inf.*)	shall we
Opa (*colloq.*)	grandpa
Schuss (*n., m.*)	shot, small quantity
Lebensfreude (*n., f.*)	enjoyment of life, "joie de vivre"
vermitteln (*v., inf.*)	let have, supply with

Everyday English

"Well, shall we let Grandpa have a shot of 'joie de vivre'?"

Ane

„Wieder 'n ‚fünfer'! Hör mal, Freundchen, ich will 'n duftes Zeugnis—also, wenn Du mir schon vorsagst, dann lern gefälligst!“

Key Words

wieder (*adv.*)	again
'n (ein)	a
fünfer	"fiver" (failing grade)
hör (*v.*, hören *inf.*)	hear
mal (einmal)	once and for all
Freundchen (*dim. of* Freund, n., m.)	little friend
will (*v.*, wollen *inf.*)	want
duftes (duft, *colloq.*)	sweet-smelling, i.e., good
Zeugnis (*n., n.*)	grade (school)
also wenn (*conj.*)	if
schon (*adv.*)	already
vorsagst (*v.*, vorsagen *inf.*)	to prompt
dann	then
lern (*v.*, lernen *inf.*)	learn, study
gefälligst (*adv.*)	please

Everyday English

"An F again! Listen, pal, I want a good grade if you let me copy from you. Next time, please study!"

Ane

„Hallo, Kumpel,—hick—du kannst wieder reinkommen—hick—die Damenwahl ist vorbei!"

Key Words

Kumpel (Kumpan, *n., m.*)	fellow
kannst (*v.,* können *inf.*)	may
wieder (*adv.*)	again
reinkommen (hereinkommen, *v., inf.*)	come in
Damenwahl (*n., f.*)	ladies' choice
vorbei (*adj.*)	finished, over
Maskenball (*n., m.*)	masked ball

Everyday English

"Hello, friend—(hic!)—you can come in now—(hic!)—ladies' choice is over."

Ane

„Mein Jott, Ilseken, was bin ich froh, nach dem verregneten Campingurlaub wieder mal in'ne trockene Bude zu kommen!"

Key Words

Mein Jott (*slang for* Mein Gott)	good gosh
Ilseken (*dim.*)	Ilse
froh (*adv.*)	glad
dem (*art.*)	the
verregneten (verregnet, *adj.*)	rained-out
Campingurlaub (*n., m.*)	camping vacation
wieder	again
mal (einmal)	once
in'ne (in eine)	in, into a
trockene (trocken, *adj.*)	dry
Bude (*n., f.*)	place, house
kommen (*v., inf.*)	come

Everyday English

"Good gosh, Ilse, am I glad to come back to a dry house after that rained-out camping vacation."

Ane

„Herr Krause, damit wir uns recht versteh'n, was jetzt auf Sie zukommt, hat absolut nichts mit dem 1. April zu tun."

Key Words

damit (*conj.*)	so that
recht (richtig)	right, correctly
versteh'n (verstehen, *v., inf.*)	understand
zukommt (*v.,* zukommen *inf.*)	come towards
absolut (*adv.*)	absolutely
tun (*v., inf.*)	do

Everyday English

"Mr. Krause, so that we understand one another, what you are about to see is NOT an April Fool's joke."

Ane

„Schule bleibt Schule—kiekste, auch hier bleiben welche sitzen."

Key Words

Tanzschule	dance school
bleibt (*v.,* bleiben *inf.*)	remain
kiekste (*colloq. for* guck mal) (*v.,* gucken *inf.*)	look
auch hier (*adv.*)	even here
welche	some
sitzen (*v., inf.*)	sit

Everyday English

"All schools are the same. Look, even here somebody's been left back."

Ane

„Bitte erfüllen Sie mir meinen letzten Wunsch.—Gehen Sie heute abend mit mir aus."

Key Words

erfüllen (*v., inf.*)	fulfill
letzten (*adj.*)	last
Wunsch (*n., m.*)	wish
gehen ... aus (*v., ausgehen inf.*)	go out
heute abend	tonight

Everyday English

"Please fulfill my last wish and go out with me tonight."

Ane

„Mal ehrlich, möchtest du bei *dem* Sauwetter draussen sein?"

Key Words

ehrlich (*adv.*)	honestly
möchtest (*v.*, mögen *inf.*)	like to
Sauwetter (*n., n.*)	bad weather (literally, "pig's weather")
draussen (*adv.*)	outside

Everyday English

"Honestly, would *you* like to be outside in this rotten weather?"

Ane

„Was seh ich da, du kriegst ja auch schon eine kahle Stelle, Peter!"

Key Words

seh (sehe) (*v.*, sehen *inf.*)   see

kriegst (*v.*, kriegen *inf.*)   get

schon (*adv.*)   already

kahle (kahl, *adj.*)   bald

Stelle (*n., f.*)   place, spot

Everyday English

"What do I see, you're already getting a bald spot, Peter!"

German–English Glossary

Note: 1. Verbs are given in the infinitive form.

2. Remember nouns are capitalized in German.

Abend evening, 82

Abmeldungen departure notice, 36

Absichten intentions, 91

absolut absolutely, 97

abziehen put on (a show), 87

ach alas, 33

ach oh, 13

alle all, 10

alle everybody, all, 69

alles everything, 59

also so, 89

also wenn if, 94

Altbau old housing, 67

Amtshandlung official act, 54

Amtsrat officer, 15

Analphabet illiterate, 13

ander other, 26

Anderen others, 5, 10

Anfang beginning, 18

anfangen begin, to do (with), 22

anfeuchten dampen, 35

Angaben data, 8

angreifen attack, 85

Angst fear, 17, 61

anhaben wear, 28

Anmeldungen registrations, 36

Anträge applications, 36

anzapfen tap, 83

Ärger anger, 30

ärgern anger, to make cross, 31

Arzt doctor, 39, 77

aufhaben wear, 34

aufhängen hang up, 26

aufhören stop, 31

aufklären enlighten, 12

aufpassen take care, 62

auftreten appear, perform, 87

Auf Wiedersehen good-bye, 35

Auge eye, 2

Ausbildung training, studies, 66

ausgehen go out, 99

ausgerechnet exactly when, 91

ausmachen switch off, 38

aussehen look, 25

aussteigen get out, disembark, 69

Autoschulden car payments, 81

Badehose bathing suit, 60

Bärenfell bearskin, 60

Baumschützer tree protectors (environmentalists), 88

Beamter bureaucrat, 14, 84

Begeisterungssturm storm of enthusiasm, 30

bei Ihnen with you, at your house, 82

erste first, 2

ersten first, 97

erster first, 6

essen eat, 22, 23

etwas something, 42

Fata Morgana mirage, 89

fehlen lack, be wrong with, 56

Fenster window, 32

Finanzminister finance minister, 73

finden find, 29

Fische fish, 75

fliegen fly, 4

Fluchtauto getaway car, 55

Fortschritt progress, 39

Frass food (mostly for animals), 88

Frau madam, 12

Frauchen little woman, 28

Freitag Friday, 59

Freundchen little friend, 94

froh glad, 96

Frühjahrsmüdigkeit spring fever, 33, 84

fühlen feel, 92

Führerschein driver's license, 65

fünfer failing grade, 94

ganz entirely, 18, 84; very, 82

Gastspiel performance, 30

Gebühren fees, 35

Geburtsdatum date of birth, 8

gefälligst if you please, 94

Gefangene prisoners, 37

gegen against, 14, 31, 60, 88

Gehaltserhöhung raise in salary, 36

gehen go, walk, jog, 65, 86

gehören belong, 88

gehorsamst obediently, 37

gell? isn't it so?, 15

genau exactly, 46

generell generally, on principle, 88

genügen to suffice, 3

geraten get into, 30

glauben believe, 16

Grönland Greenland, 60

gross great, 17

Gruppe group, 7

Gruppen-Therapie group therapy, 7

gucken look, 32, 98

gut good, 20, 25, 34

Guten Tag good day, hello, 35

Haarwuchs hair-growing, 24

hallo hello, 31

Haus house, 40

Heiligabend Christmas Eve, 87

Heiterkeit hilarity, 32

Heizöl heating oil, 41

Herbst autumn, 48

herein come in, 35

hereinkommen come in, 95

herunter down, 89

heute today, 7

heute abend tonight, 99

Tierzählung animal census, 76

tragen carry, wear, 27, 53

treffen hit, 84

treiben practice, 22

trinken drink, 19, 22

Trinkgeld tip, 80

trocken dry, 96

Trubel excitement, 32

Truppenübungsplatz army drill ground, 45

tun do, 14, 20, 97

Typ guy, person, 78, 87

typisch typical, 42

überall everywhere, 34

übersetzen translate, 79

U-Boot submarine, 62

Uhr hour, 49

Ummeldungen moving notices, 36

umsonst free of charge, 68

umweltfreundlich environmentally friendly, 70

und so weiter et cetera, 8

Unsichtbare invisible man, 9

unten downstairs, 12

Unterricht lesson, 71

unverzichtbar indispensable, 77

Vaterunser The Lord's Prayer, 3

Verbot prohibition, 70

vererben leave (to heirs), 40

verkaufen sell, 40

verkehrt reverse, 34

verkehrt rum upside down, 26

vermeiden avoid, 22

vermitteln let have, supply with, 93

vernünftig reasonably, 22

verregnet rained-out, 96

verstehen understand, 21, 97

Verzeihung excuse me, 13

verzichten do without, 36

viel much, 22, 74, 81

vielleicht perhaps, 91

vom from, 11

von dem from, 11

vorbei over, finished, 95

vorerst for the time being, 3

vorher before, 92

vorig previous, 30

vorsagen prompt, 94

Wachhund watchdog, 44

Wagen car, 78

wahr true, real, 74

warten wait, 28, 50

Wartezimmer waiting room, 50

was für ein what kind of, 66

Wasserflöhe waterfleas, 76

wegen because of, 44

Weihnachtsmann Santa Claus, 34

weil because, 84

welche some, 98

wenn when, 32

werden become, 64, 66, 73, 77, 83, 90

English-German Glossary

Note: 1. German verbs are given in the infinitive form.
2. Remember nouns are capitalized in German.

a bit bisschen, 74

absolutely absolut, 97

advice Rat, 27

again wieder, 28, 88, 94, 95, 96

against gegen, 14, 31, 60, 88

airline pilot Linienpilot, 16

alas ach, 33

all alle, 10

along lang, 86

always immer, 5, 46, 77

anger Ärger, 30

anger, make cross ärgern, 31

animal census Tierzählung, 76

animal experiments Tierversuche, 1

appear, perform auftreten, 87

applications Anträge, 36

army drill ground Truppenübungsplatz, 45

as a twosome zu zweit, 81

at last endlich, 31, 41

attack angreifen, 85

at your house bei Ihnen, 82

autumn Herbst, 48

avoid vermeiden, 22

bad weather Sauwetter, 52, 100

bald kahl, 101

bare, naked bloss, 2

bark bellen, 44

bathing suit Badehose, 60

be able to, can können, 2

be allowed to dürfen, 36

bearskin Bärenfell, 60

beautiful, nicely schön, 5, 41, 48

beauty contest Schönheits-Wettbewerb, 72

because weil, 84

because of wegen, 44

become werden, 64, 66, 73, 77, 83, 90

be correct stimmen, 9

beef Rindfleisch, 23

before vorher, 92

begin, to do (with) anfangen, 22

beginning Anfang, 18

believe glauben, 16

belong gehören, 88

blood reserves Blutkonserven, 83

bureaucrat Beamter, 14, 84

camping vacation Campingurlaub, 96

can, be able to können, 10, 13, 40, 52, 95

car Wagen, 78

car payments Autoschulden, 81

carry, wear tragen, 27, 53

caseworker Sachbearbeiter, 36

charming, very nice reizend, 82

chatter klappern, 75

children's beds Kinderbetten, 51

choice Belieben, 80

Christmas Eve Heiligabend, 87

class Klasse, 16

climb steigen, 89

coal Kohlen, 41

colleague Kollege, 2

collect zusammenbringen, 90

come kommen, 12, 31, 34, 91, 96

come in herein, 35; hereinkommen, 95

come towards zukommen, 97

complaints Beschwerden, 39

consultation hours Sprechstunde, 39

copy from vorsagen, 94

correct richtig, 78, 97

count nachzählen, 76

create schaffen, 18

dachshund Dackel, 72

dampen anfeuchten, 35

dance school Tanzschule, 98

data Angaben, 8

date of birth Geburtsdatum, 8

days Tage, 48

dear liebe, 12

department stores Kaufhäusern, 87

departure notice Abmeldungen, 36

describe schildern, 39

detect entdecken, 2

diabetic Diabetiker, 13

die sterben, 17

discover entdecken, 2

disembark aussteigen, 69

district office Bezirksamt, 35

disturb stören, 54

dive springen, 62

do machen, 1, 18, 55, 64; tun, 14, 20, 97

do without verzichten, 36

doctor Arzt, 39, 77

dog Hund, 11

dog psychologist Hundepsychologen, 27

doorbells Klingelknöpfe, 31

double-decker zweistöckig, 52

down herunter, 89; runter, 11, 31

down from von dem, 11

downstairs unten, 12

drink trinken, 19, 22

driver's license Führerschein, 65

dry trocken, 84

earth Erde, 18

easier leichter, 81

easily leicht, 15

Easter Ostern, 45

eat essen, 22, 23

elephant Elefant, 89

enjoyment of life
Lebensfreude, 93

enlighten aufklären, 12

entirely ganz, 18, 84

environmentalists
Baumschützer, 88

environmentally friendly
umweltfreundlich, 70

et cetera und so weiter, 8

even sogar, 75

evening Abend, 82

everybody alle, 69

everything alles, 59

everywhere überall, 34

exactly genau, 46

exactly when ausgerechnet, 91

examiner Prüfer, 16

exchange tauschen, 60

excitement Trubel, 32

excuse me entschuldigen, 21;
Verzeihung, 13

eye Auge, 2

failing grade fünfer, 94

fat one Dicker, 83

fear Angst, 17, 61

feel fühlen, 92

fees Gebühren, 35

fellow Kumpel, 95

fiancee Braut, 31

finance minister
Finanzminister, 73

find finden, 29

finished vorbei, 95

finish line Ziel, 90

first erste, ersten, erster, 2, 6, 97

fish Fische, 75

flag Holz, 90

fly fliegen, 4

food (mostly for animals)
Frass, 88

for zu dem, 86

for the time being vorerst, 3

for two people zu zweit, 81

for weeks wochenlang, 87

for years jahrelang, 32

free of charge umsonst, 68

Friday Freitag, 59

frighten erschrecken, 27

from von dem, 11

fulfill erfüllen, 99

funny witzig, 29

further nähere, 8

gasoline Benzin, 68

generally generell, 88

get bekommen, 47; holen, 27;
kriegen, 101

getaway car Fluchtauto, 55

get into geraten, 30

get out aussteigen, 69

giant slalom Riesenslalom, 90

give schenken, 86

glad froh, 96

go gehen, 65, 86

good gut, 20, 25, 34

good-bye Auf Wiedersehen, 35

good day Guten Tag, 35

good gosh Mein Jott, 96

go out ausgehen, 99

grade Zeugnis, 94

grandpa Opa, 93

great gross, 17

Greenland Grönland, 60

group Gruppe, 7

group therapy Gruppen-
Therapie, 7

guy Typ, 87

hair-growing Haarwuchs, 24

hang up aufhängen, 26

headache Kopfschmerz, 92

hear hören, 83, 94

heating oil Heizöl, 41

heat wave Hitzewelle, 60

heaven Himmel, 18

hello Guten Tag, 35; hallo, 31

helpful hilfsbereit, 36

here hier, 39, 63, 98

hibernation Winterschlaf, 33

higher, more expensive
teurer, 68

hilarity Heiterkeit, 32

hit treffen, 84

hold on, stick it out
durchhalten, 15

honestly ehrlich, 81, 100

hospital Krankenhaus, 56

hour Uhr, 49

house Haus, 40

how wie, 86

human being Mensch, 78

humor Humor, 91

ice Eis, 53

ideal ideal, 57

if wenn, 94

if you please gefälligst, 94

illiterate Analphabet, 13

Ilse Ilseken, 96

imagine meinen, 12

indispensable unverzichtbar,
77

intentions Absichten, 91

in the im, 89

into zu der, 77

into the in das, 68

invisible man Unsichtbare, 9

isn't it so? gell?, 15

job counseling
Berufsberatung, 66

jog gehen, 65

"joie de vivre" Lebensfreude,
93

jokes Scherze, 43

jubilation Jubel, 32

jump springen, 62

know wissen, 4, 28, 86

know the ropes wissen wie's
lang geht, 86

lack, be wrong with fehlen,
56

ladies' choice Damenwahl,
86

last letzten, 99

learn lernen, 94

leave (to heirs) vererben,
40

self selber, 44, 76; selbst, 4
sell verkaufen, 40
serious ernst, 91
seven sieben, 51
several zig, 87
shade schatten, 29
shall wollen, 93
shorter kürzere, 72
shot schiessen, 89, 93
small quantity Schuss, 93
should dürfen, 3
silencer Schalldämpfer, 58
since seit, 16; seitdem, 88
single room Einzelzimmer, 51
sister dear Schwesterherz, 86
sit sitzen, 29, 98
skirt Rock, 28
sky Himmel, 18
sleeping pill Schlafmittel, 38
smoke rauchen, 22, 61
smoker's cough
  Raucherhusten, 47
snow tires Winterreifen, 64
Snow White Schneewittchen,
  51
so also, 89
some welche, 98
someday einmal, 73
something etwas, 42
so that damit, 40, 97
speak sprechen, 39
special bus Sonderbus, 52
sponsor widmen, 24
spring fever
  Frühjahrsmüdigkeit, 33, 84

stamp (something)
  stempeln, 35
starving artist
  Hungerkünstler, 25
stop aufhoren, 31; lassen, 43;
  stoppen, 58
storm of enthusiasm
  Begeisterungssturm, 30
strike streiken, 36, 55
strong kräftig, 34
studies Ausbildung, 66
study lernen, 94; studieren, 40
stylish modern, 28
submarine U-Boot, 62
such solch, 78
suffice genügen, 3
sun Sonne, 29
supply with vermitteln, 93
support Stütze, 77
sweet-smelling (good) duft,
  94
switch off ausmachen, 38
take nehmen, 92; machen, 37
take care aufpassen, 62
take notice of kümmern, 32
take out entnehmen, 39
tap anzapfen, 83
target Ziel, 84
tasteless lasch, 88
teeth Zähnen, 75
terminal Endstation, 69
that dass, 62, 64
the dem, 96
then dann, 94
thirteenth dreizehnte, 59

English-German Subject Index
Titles, People and Characteristics

all, everybody alle, 10, 69

dear liebe, 12

fat guy Dicker, 83

fellow Kumpel, 95

fiancee Braut, 31

Grandpa Opa, 93

group Gruppe, 7

group therapy
Gruppen-Therapie, 7

guy, person Typ, 78, 87

hilarity, laughter Heiterkeit,
32

humor Humor, 91

illiterate Analphabet, 13

Ilse Ilseken, 96

invisible man Unsichtbare,
9

ladies' choice Damenwahl,
95

little friend Freundchen, 94

**little woman (dog's
owner)** Frauchen, 28

Lord's Prayer Vaterunser, 3

lout Lümmel, 85

Madam Frau, 12

man Mann, 88

man, human being Mensch,
78

no one keiner, 32

one man, 66, 86

others Anderen 5, 10

prisoners Gefangene, 37

self selbst, selber, 4, 44, 76

sister dear Schwesterherz,
86

Snow White Schneewittchen,
51

starving artist
Hungerkünstler, 25

winner Sieger, 90

young jung, 17, 91

Officials, Bureaucracy

applications Anträge, 36

army drill ground
Truppenübungsplatz, 45

bureaucrat Beamter, 14, 84

caseworker Sachbearbeiter,
36

complaints Beschwerden,
39

data Angaben, 8

departure notice Abmeldung,
36

district office Bezirksamt,
35

finance minister
Finanzminister, 73

moving notice Ummeldung,
36

officer Amtsrat, 13

official act Amtshandlung,
54

prohibition Verbot, 70

registration Anmeldung, 36
report melden, 37
rubber stamp Stempel, 35

stamp (v.) stempeln, 35
traffic-ticket writer
  Strafzettelschreiber, 54

Actions

add to hinzukommen, 42
aim, target Ziel, 84, 90
appear, perform auftreten, 87
attack angreifen, 85
avoid vermeiden, 22
bark bellen, 44
become werden, 64, 66, 73, 77, 83, 90
believe glauben, 16
belong to gehören, 88
bring together
  zusammenbringen, 90
carry, wear tragen, 27, 53
chatter klappern, 75
climb steigen, 89
come kommen, 12, 31, 34, 91, 96
come towards zukommen, 97
create schaffen, 18
describe schildern, 39
detect, discover entdecken, 2
die sterben, 17
disturb stören, 54
do tun, 14, 20, 97
do machen, 1, 13, 18, 37, 55, 64
do without verzichten, 36
exchange tauschen, 60
explain, enlighten
  aufklären, 12

find finden, 29
fly fliegen, 14
get bekommen, 47; holen, 27; kriegen, 101
get into, meet with geraten, 30
get out aussteigen, 69
give a present schenken, 86
go gehen, 65, 86
go out ausgehen, 99
hang up aufhängen, 26
hear, listen hören, 83, 94
hold on, stick it out
  durchhalten, 15
jump, dive springen, 62
leave (to heirs) vererben, 40
let lassen, 88
look aussehen, 25; gucken, 32, 98
meet, hit treffen, 84
moisten, dampen
  anfeuchten, 35
moveable beweglich, 84
open öffnen, 49
participate in a celebration
  mitgefeiert, 34
pay zahlen, 81
pour schütten, 68
practice treiben, 22
press drücken, 31

prompt   vorsagen, 94

put on (a show)   abziehen, 87

result in   ergeben, 22

say   sagen, 35, 86

see, view   sehen, 52, 74, 89, 101

shoot   schiessen, 89

sit   sitzen, 29, 98

speak   sprechen, 39

sponsor   widmen, 24

stop   aufhören, 31; lassen, 43; stoppen, 58

strike   streiken, 36, 55

supply with   vermitteln, 93

switch off   ausmachen, 38

take   nehmen, 92

take care   aufpassen, 62

take notice of   kümmern, 32

take out   entnehmen, 39

tap   anzapfen, 83

thrown in   einwerfen, 39

translate   übersetzen, 79

wait   warten, 28

wear, carry   tragen, 27, 53

will   werden, 20

write   schreiben, 13

When, How Much

a bit   bisschen, 74

absolutely   absolut, 97

again   wieder, 28, 88, 94, 95, 96

always   immer 5, 46, 77

at last   endlich, 31, 41

before   vorher, 92

begin   anfangen, 22

beginning   Anfang, 18

count, check   nachzählen, 76

days   Tage, 48

enormous   enorm, 22

entirely   ganz, 18, 46, 84

even   auch, 87

exactly   ausgerechnet, 91

first   erst, 7, 97

for the time being   vorerst, 3

for weeks   wochenlang, 87

for years   jahrelang, 32

Friday   Freitag, 59

further   nähere, 8

great, large   gross, 17

hour   Uhr, 49

last   letzten, 99

long   lang, 33

longer   länger, 31

long time   lange, 50

many   zig, 87

moderately   mässig, 19

modern times   Neuzeit, 38

more   mehr, 17, 23, 65, 77

most   meist, 90

much   viel, 22, 74, 81

narrow   eng, 28

next   nächste, 7

normally   normalerweise, 4

nothing, not   nichts, 4, 13

now   jetzt, 17, 32, 33, 92

once einmal, 86, 94, 96; mal, 40, 88

one eins 5

only bloss, 72

only one Einzige, 47

particularly besonders, 84

previous vorig, 30

quickly schnell, 83

scarce knapp, 83

shot, small quantity Schuss, 93

since seit, 16; seitdem, 88

some welche, 98

some day einmal, 73

thirteenth dreizehnte, 59

Thursdays Donnerstags, 49

time Zeit, 22, 64

today heute, 7

tonight heute abend, 99

two people, as a twosome zu zweit, 81

until bis, 15, 49

very sehr, 17, 18

when wann, 16

Where

against gegen, 14, 31, 60, 88

along lang, 29

at your house bei Ihnen, 82

come in herein(kommen), 35, 95

down herunter, 11, 31, 89

downstairs unten, 12

even here auch hier, 98

everywhere überall, 34

from, of von, 11

here hier, 39, 63, 98

how wie, 86

in the im, 89

into a in eine, 96

into the in das, 68

long lang, 33

on it drauf, 34, 64

outside draussen, 61, 100

place, spot Stelle, 101

reverse verkehrt, 34

shorter kürzere, 72

stay, remain bleiben, 98

to, into zur, 15, 77

upside down verkehrt rum, 26

What Things?

everything alles, 59

flag Holz, 90

for zum, 86

mask Maske, 34

mirage Fata Morgana, 89

muzzle Maulkorb, 27

no kein, keine, keinen, 27, 47, 61, 65

other ander, 26

pictures Bilder, 26

silencer Schalldämpfer, 70

something etwas, 42

How Is It? Feelings, Thoughts, Conditions

Exclamations!

alas   ach, 33

excuse me   Entschuldigen Sie, 21; Verzeihung, 13

good-bye   Auf Wiedersehen, 35

good gosh   Mein Jott, 96

hello   hallo, 31

hello, good day   Guten Tag, 35

honestly   ehrlich, 81, 100

if you please   gefälligst, 94

isn't it so?   gell?, 15

is that correct?   Stimmt's?, 9

nonsense   Blödsinn, 59

oh   ach, 13

Health and Body

attack   angreifen, 85

bare, naked   bloss, 2

bald   kahl, 101

bathing suit   Badehose, 60

bearskin   Bärenfell, 60

blood reserves   Blutkonserven, 83

consultation hours   Sprechstunde, 39

diabetic   Diabetiker, 13

doctor   Arzt, 39, 77

dog psychiatrist   Hundepsychologen, 27

eye   Auge, 2

examiner   Prüfer, 16

hair-growing   Haarwuchs, 24

headache   Kopfschmerz, 92

hospital   Krankenhaus, 56

legs   Beine, 72

medical   medizinisch, 39

medical certificate   Krankenschein, 39

nonsmoker   Nichtraucher, 61

nurse   Krankenschwester, 77

pills   Tablette, 92

practice   Praxis, 39

prescriptions   Rezepte, 3, 39

remedy   Mittel, 24

skirt   Rock, 28

sleeping pill   Schlafmittel, 38

smoke   rauchen, 22, 61

smoker's cough   Raucherhusten, 47

teeth   Zähne, 75

violently   tätlich, 85

waiting room   Wartezimmer, 50

wear   anhaben, aufhaben, 28, 34; tragen, 27

Food and Drink

beef   Rindfleisch, 23

drink   trinken, 19, 22

eat   essen, 22, 23

food (mostly for animals)   Frass, 88

menu   Speisekarte, 79

salt   Salz, 88

tasteless   lasch, 88

waiter   Kellner, 57

Quality of Life

advancement, progress
Fortschritt, 39

class Klasse, 16

enjoyment Lebensfreude, 93

fulfill erfüllen, 99

grade report Zeugnis, 94

ideal ideal, 52

jubilation Jubel, 32

lesson Unterricht, 71

life expectancy
Lebenserwartung, 22

power plant
Elektrizitätswerk, 42

studies, training
Ausbildung, 66

study studieren, 40

study, learn lernen, 94

suffice genügen, 3

support Stütze, 77

Nature and Weather

animal census Tierzählung, 76

animal experiments
Tierversuche, 1

autumn Herbst, 48

bad weather Sauwetter, 52

dry trocken, 96

earth Erde, 18

environmentalists
Baumschützer, 88

environmentally friendly
umweltfreundlich, 70

fish Fische, 75

Greenland Grönland, 60

heat wave Hitzewelle, 60

hibernation Winterschlaf, 33

ice Eis, 53

meadow Wiese, 24

Mount Vesuvius Vesuv, 47

rained-out verregnet, 96

sea Meer, 68

shade Schatten, 29

sky Himmel, 18

sun Sonne, 29

waterfleas Wasserflöhe, 76

weather Wetter, 41

At Home

children's beds Kinderbetten, 51

coal Kohlen, 41

dachshund Dackel, 72

dog Hund, 11

doorbells Klingelknöpfe, 31

heating oil Heizöl, 41

house Haus, 40

old housing Altbau, 67

modernization
Modernisierung, 67

place, house Bude, 96

watchdog Wachhund, 44

window Fenster, 32

Earning a Living and Shopping

colleague Kollege, 2

department stores
Kaufhäuser, 87

expensive (more expensive)
teurer, 68

fees Gebühren, 35

free of charge umsonst, 68

job counseling
Berufsberatung, 66

purchase Kauf, 78

raise in salary
Gehaltserhöhung, 36

retirement Pensionierung, 15

tip Trinkgeld, 80

Holiday, Leisure Time and Travel

airline pilot Linienpilot, 14

camping vacation
Campingurlaub, 96

car Wagen, 78

car payments Autoschulden,
81

celebrate mitfeiern, 34

Christmas Eve Heiligabend,
87

competition Wettbewerb, 72

dance school Tanzschule,
96

double-decker zweistöckig,
52

driver's license
Führerschein, 65

Easter Ostern, 45

excitement Trubel, 32

gasoline Benzin, 68

getaway car Fluchtauto, 55

giant slalom Riesenslalom,
90

low flights Tiefflüge, 58

masked ball Maskenball, 95

Mother's Day Muttertag, 86

night flight Nachtflug, 70

park guardian Parkwächter,
85

performance Gastspiel, 30

Santa Claus
Weihnachtsmann, 34

single room Einzelzimmer, 51

snow tires Winterreifen, 64

special bus Sonderbus, 52

took part in a celebration
mitgefeiert, 34

terminal Endstation, 69

vacation Betriebsferien, 44

Connectors

because weil, 27

because of wegen, 44

et cetera und so weiter, 8

even sogar, 75

if wenn, also wenn, 94

like wie, 10, 46, 72, 92

of that davor, 17

only nur, 14

so also, 89

so that damit, 40, 97

such solch, 78

that dass, 62, 64

the dem, 96